Exploring the Peak District

by

Peter Grayson

Dalesman Books
1987

The Dalesman Publishing Company Ltd.,
Clapham, Lancaster, LA2 8EB.
First published by Grayson Publications
This edition, © Peter Grayson 1987

ISBN: 0 85206 892 1

Printed by Fretwell & Cox Ltd.,
Goulbourne Street, Keighley, West Yorkshire BD21 1PZ.

Contents

    Introduction 5
1. The Hope Valley and Northern Moors 6
2. Chatsworth House, Eyam and Tideswell 12
3. Bakewell, Buxton and Ashford 19
4. Bakewell, Youlgreave and Flagg 24
5. Haddon, Birchover and Hartington 29
6. Matlock, Crich and Wirksworth 34
7. Ashbourne, Dovedale and Manifold Valley 41
    Index 48

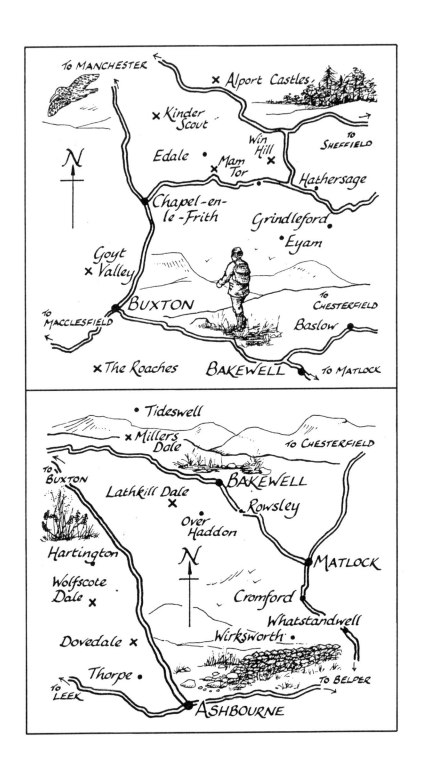

Introduction

WELCOME to Derbyshire's Peak District. The natural beauty of the area — the open moors and the picturesque villages — along with its rich history, art, customs, sporting and outdoor facilities make it the ideal playground in which to relax. Indeed, 15 million people live within 50 miles of Bakewell, and there is something here for all of them, as well as the holidaymakers and tourists who come every year.

I have tried to cater for every need by dividing the region into seven areas, each of which can be covered in one day. There is a walk described in each section. This can either be included in the outing, or done separately. The directions are based on the maps generally available. These are:
1. The Ordnance Survey's Peak District Tourist Map.
2. The White Peak. O.S. Outdoor Leisure Map No. 24.
3. The Dark Peak. O.S. Map. 1:25,000 series.

For those without a car, there are good connecting bus services. There is a rail link from Derby to Matlock as well as the Hope Valley line. It is possible to hire bicycles in some places, and there is even a horse-drawn tram service in Chesterfield.

Walkers should always be prepared for a change in the weather, so go well prepared — especially over the moors around Edale and on the Pennine Way. Don't go out on your own without telling someone where you will re-appear, and follow the advice of the Peak District Wardens. I have chosen the easier, more spectacular, walks in each area, but there are many more to be tried out. Other activities include rock-climbing, canoeing, caving, hang gliding and conventional gliding. Join a club, if you want to do these.

More information can be obtained from the National Park Caravan, which is parked at most of the festivities, and from the Tourist Information Centres at Matlock Bath, Buxton, Bakewell, Ashbourne, Bolsover, Chesterfield and Derby.

Peter Grayson

Opposite: Sketch maps of northern and southern Peakland

1. The Hope Valley and Northern Moors

Fox House — Hathersage — Ladybower — Bamford — Brough — Hope — Castleton. 25 miles.

Recommended walks: "Short Walks starting in Hathersage" by Rev M. Hulbert, Philip Key and Tom Tomlinson.

THE roads from Sheffield (A625), Chesterfield (B6055) and Bakewell (A6011) all meet at Fox House, an attractive public house at the foot of Burbage and Totley Moors near Sheffield. The Sheffield buses, Nos. 208 and 308 to Buxton, No. 272 to Castleton, and No. 240 to Bakewell all stop and meet here. This is part of the "Golden Frame" around Sheffield, and leads to one of the most spectacular areas of the Peak Dsitrict. Just across the road is . . .

The Longshaw Estate. Formerly a Shooting Lodge belonging to the Dukes of Rutland, it is now owned by the National Trust. The famous Sheepdog Trials are held here each year, during the first week in September.

Take the A625 towards the Hope Valley, and notice the two flat-topped mountains on the right. The distant one is Higger Tor, the near one is Carl's Wark — the site of an Iron Age fortress. Cross over the bridge and notice the curious rock formation on the right-hand side of the road. This is the Toad's Mouth. Looked at from the correct angle, it is easy to see why. Continue along the A625 to the . . .

Surprise View. Pass between the rocks on the edge of the moor and the whole of the Hope Valley is set out before you. The type of weather for the day can easily be assessed from here. Down the hill now, pass the Millstone Hotel, and into . . .

Hathersage. Note the view of the church on the right and turn this way, just before entering the village. Go as far as The Scotsman's Pack and turn left up the hill to the church of St. Michael and All Angels. There is an adequate car park with a convenient pathway across the churchyard. A look at the extensive bookstall in the church (obtain a copy of the Walks Book here) shows the village's connection with Charlotte Bronte.

Charlotte came to stay with her friend Ellen Nussey, who lived at the Old Vicarage. This is where she wrote her novel *Jane Eyre* and nearly all the village and its surroundings are featured in her work. The name of the local

Hathersage Church

district of Morton was changed to Norton for her village name, and Jane's surname was taken from that of the local family dating back to William the Conqueror.

The tombs of the Eyre family are in the chancel and are covered in brasses dating back to the 15th century. The Eyres were said to have given "air" to William at a critical point in the Battle of Hastings and were granted an estate in Derbyshire in return. The tombs start with that of Robert and Joan Eyre and their family, dated 1459. They had many children and there are brasses commemorating other members of the family. They built their houses around the district, all wthin sight of their previous family home. Replicas of the brasses and some rubbing equipment are available in the vestry for use in return for a small fee.

The church also contains two Austrian chairs, used by Queen Victoria and her consort for the opening of Liverpool Town Hall. These were given to the church, as the stone for the building was quarried locally.

Little John's Grave is in the churchyard. An old tradition said that Robin Hood's accomplice was buried beneath a cottage near the church. When some digging was done, amongst other things, a thigh bone measuring 32 inches long was found. These remains were eventually reburied in the churchyard and a tree was planted at each end of the grave, at a distance representing the height of Little John. An old gentleman, who lives in a cottage nearby the original one, keeps the churchyard tidy and is a mine of information.

Now rejoin the main road into the village, down the hill to the road

North Lees Hall

junction opposite the George Hotel. Notice the old Victorian lamp-post now used as a fingerboard, but continue a short way along the A625. Take the first right out of the village — up Jaggers Lane, and then right again where there is a signpost to Stanage Moor. Up here as far as Birley Lane. Turn right down here, and stop just over the bridge, just before the National Park Camping Site (for tents only) at . . .

North Lees. Charlotte Bronte changed "North to Thorn" and, knowing that "Lees" meant "Fields", made her "Thornfield Hall". It was here that Mrs. Rochester jumped from the roof to her death, in the novel. The Hall is no longer open to the public.

Retrace your steps way up Birley Lane, and turn right at the top towards Stanage Moor. Progress up here, noting the fine view of the Hope Valley to the left, pass Gatehouse Lane, followed by a left turn marked "Ladybower". Note the fine views again, and continue as far as the A6013. Turn right, pass the Yorkshire Bridge Inn and arrive at . . .

Ladybower Reservoir. Started in 1935, it was officially opened by King George VI and Queen Elizabeth on the 25th September 1945. It supplies water to the Midland cities as far away as Birmingham, and was a considerable achievement in its day. Unfortunately, the villages of Derwent and Ashopton were lost below the water level. Continue along here to the A57. Turn left, cross the Ashopton Viaduct and then turn right, marked . . .

Derwent Valley. The road passes alongside the upper part of the Ladybower, and the Derwent and Howden Reservoirs are further up this road which has no exit after the Derwent Reservoir. Howden Reservoir was used by Dr. Barnes Wallis and "The Dambusters" Squadron of the RAF, as a practice site during the Second World War. There is a memorial to a Sheepdog called "Tip" up here. He stood by the body of his master for 15 weeks after he perished in a snow blizzard on the moors above. Turn round now and follow the signs back to . . .

Bamford. The present church of St. John the Baptist was designed by William Butterfield, a famous Victorian architect who, amongst other things, designed the chapel at Rugby School.

Rejoin the A625 at the Marquis of Grandby, taking the right turn. Go as far as the Travellers' Rest, and then turn left along the B6049 to . . .

Brough. By the side of the bridge, there is a footpath leading to Hope, which crosses over the rectangular remains of the Roman Fort "Anavio". This was built as a station on the old Roman road called Batham Gate, running from Templeborough in South Yorkshire to the baths at Buxton. Several interesting items are preserved in their Museum. (see Tour 3). Return to the A625 and turn left for . . .

Hope. Famous for its Show held on August Bank Holiday Monday and its well dressings held on the Saturday nearest to the Feast of St. Peter, the 29th June. The shaft of a Saxon Cross is in the church yard.

The road to Edale leaves the village by the Bull's Head. Take note of the two hills on each side of this road. The one on the left is Lose Hill and the one on the right is Win Hill. These are named after the defeated and victorious armies' positions taken before an ancient battle, which took place here over 1500 years ago.

Leave the village by the A625, pass the National Park Caravan Site on the right, before entering . . .

Castleton. At the head of the Hope Valley, this village typifies the Peak District. It is surrounded by a crescent of hills rising over 1500 feet. Here limestone meets the shales and the gritstones, the oily materials from the shales permeating the crystals of the fluorspar in the limestone to produce the world famous "Blue John".

Some say that Blue John was so called to distinguish it from Black Jack, a mineral of zinc found locally. However, it is more likely to have come from the French "Blue at Jaune", meaning "blue and yellow" — as the mineral

The Blue John Craft Shop, Castleton

also contains yellow impurities and French prisoners from the Napoleonic Wars were made to work the mines and build the walls around here. Vases made from Blue John were found in the ruins of Pompeii, and there are several in the Vatican Museum. Finely worked pieces are still presented to royalty when they visit the county. There are some fine collections to be seen in the village — especially the Ollershaw Collection. Many shops in the village sell jewellery and ornaments made from this semi-precious stone.

There is a lot more to see and do here. Apart from their Well Dressing, they still commemorate the restoration of Charles II in 1660. It is celebrated on Garland Day, May 29th, when the Morris Dancers lead a procession through the village as far as the Square. There they dance round the maypole and hoist the Garland to the top of the church tower.

There is a good Youth Hostel in the village Square, and . . .

Peveril Castle stands to the south, high above the village. This was started by William Peveril (of the Peak), a natural son of William the Conqueror. King Henry II erected the keep in 1176, but it is now maintained by the Department of the Environment. Access to the castle is by an alleyway at the top right-hand side of the village square. It is open to the public from 9.30 am to 6.30 pm each day, except on Sunday mornings during the winter, when it also closes at 4.30 pm. There is a small charge and several guide books are sold.

Leaving the square by a street locally known as "The Stones", pass by the fish and chip shop, cross the bridge and turn immediately left — it is labelled . . .

Peak Cavern. The largest natural cavern in Britain, it is entirely lit by electric light (tallow and wax candles are out). It is the property of the Duchy of Lancaster, and tours leave every 15 minutes during the season. The Cavern opens at 10.30 am and is suitable for all ages.

Walk back by the trout stream and the alleyways, and pick one of the many cafes, or public houses, providing refreshment. Look round the gift shops for a suitable souvenir.

There is a choice of three more underground caverns, all containing Blue John, to be visited. These are:

Treak Cliff Cavern — further up the A625 (which is now permanently closed due to the irreparable subsidence at the foot of the Shivering Mountain). However the cavern is open and well worth visiting.

Speedwell Cavern — again further up the A625, but this time turn left up the Winnats Pass (it is well signposted). This cavern contains some surprises, including an underground waterfall being swallowed by a "bottomless pit". It is all well lit and leaves an unforgetable impression.

Blue John Cavern is reached via the Winnats Pass and two right turns. There is a magnificent view down the valley from here, with Rushup Edge on the left and Mam Tor (the Mother Mountain) behind. The cavern contains veins of Blue John along with stalactites hanging from the ceilings and stalagmites rising from the ground.

For those with any time, and energy left, there is a footpath to the top of Mam Tor, where the remains of another Iron Age Fort can be seen.

2. Chatsworth House, Eyam and Tideswell

Bakewell — Pilsley — Chatsworth — Baslow — Stoney Middleton — Eyam — Great Hucklow — Tideswell — Litton — Wardlow — The Longstones — Hassop. 32 miles.

Recommended walk: "The Monsal Trail" — National Park Fact Finder Trail. (from the Information Centre, Bakewell).

Bakewell is the hub of the Peak District, with over 20 bus routes servicing this ancient market town. Famous for its Pudding, its annual Show and its Bank Holiday markets, it provides everything for the tourist. The Bakewell Pudding was first made by accident in the kitchens of the Rutland Arms Hotel, in 1889, and the Show is held for two days, starting on the first Wednesday in August.

The Peak District National Park Information Centre, housed in the Old Market Hall, shows just what the Peak District as to offer — wide open limestone and gritstone moorlands cut by beautiful dales and dotted with quaint villages full of ancient customs. There are so many historic houses and other popular places of interest in the area that a computer is now employed to provide all the information. Press a button for "Historic Houses", and out come all the details. The exhibition covers all the activities which go on in the Peak. These include the caverns which are open to the public, lists of places where bicycles may be hired, etc. Many leaflets are available, including an accommodation and catering guide and a list of events in the Peak District. (More about Bakewell in Tours 3 and 4).

Take the A619 towards Sheffield and Chesterfield, and go as far as the B6048 turning to . . .

Pilsley. Largely owned by the Chatsworth Estate, who have their Farm Shop here. This is on the right as you enter the village, and is part of the 9th Duke of Devonshire's Shire Horse Stud Farm, built in 1910. This has now been converted into workshops and was recently opened by the 11th Duke. Apart from the extensive Farm Shop, which provides something for everyone, the workshops are engaged in upholstery, ceramics, art design, picture framing, etc.

Returning to the B6048, turn right and note the view of the Hunting Tower in Stand Wood, to the left as you approach the B6012. Take the right turning here and go down the hill into . . .

Chatsworth House

Edensor. This village is part of the Chatsworth Estate. It originally stood lower down on the left-hand side of the road, extending as far as the entrance to the house, but only Park Cottage remains there now. In 1839, the 6th Duke decided to move the village out of sight of the House. He engaged a young architect, John Robertson from Derby, who offered the Duke his book of "models", new designs which all architects had to prepare before qualifying. These were based on several styles of continental architecture, and the Duke liked them so much that he had one of each. The Duke then engaged Sir Gilbert Scott to rebuild the earlier 14th century church, which, fortunately, stood in the right place. Only the spire is visible from the House. The church contains many of the Cavendish memorials, including those of Henry and William Cavendish, sons of Bess of Hardwick.

The late President Kennedy's sister Kathleen is buried in the churchyard. She was married to the 10th Duke's elder son, but both he and his young wife were killed during the Second World War. There is a small plaque commemorating the various visits made by members of the Kennedy family, including that by John Kennedy whilst he was the American President.

The village Post Office includes the excellent Stables' Tearooms, where good quality home made cooking is served with a smile. They have their own car park.

Out of the village now, and off to . . .

Chatsworth House — "The Palace of the Peak" and home of the Duke and Duchess of Devonshire. It is open to the public everyday from the end of March to the end of October, from 11.30 am to 4.30 pm, with the gardens open until 5.00 pm. The only restrictions are during the Country Fair at August Bank Holiday, and during the Horse Trials in early October. At these times the House and Gardens are only open to visitors to the events taking place in the Park. There is something to please everyone at Chatsworth. The best way of finding out about it is to go and see for yourself as a hundred books could not contain it all.

After seeing the House and Gardens, drive south through the Park, noting the fine views and, perhaps, seeing one of the herds of deer, to the . . .

Chatsworth Garden Centre at Calton Lees. There is a large car park at the end of the Park here, as well as the one in the centre itself. A large selection of top quality plants, garden sundries, furniture and gifts are offered for sale. Most of the centre is covered over, especially useful when the weather is wet, and there is a coffee shop. It is open seven days a week, from 10.30 am to 6.00 pm, but closes at 4.30 pm from October until February.

Retrace your way back through the Park, again noting the view to the right, and go as far as . . .

Baslow. Take the second exit from the roundabout as far as Goose Green at Nether End. There is a good car park here, and it is a good place for a stroll round — over the old bridge by the artists' cottages. It may be Well Dressing Day in early July, or the Morris Men may be dancing in August.

The main feature at this end of the village is the Cavendish Hotel. Originally the Peacock Hotel and owned by the Duke of Rutland, it passed into the Cavendish Family about 1830. It was extensively restored in the early 1970s, when most of the original character was preserved and several items were imported from Chatsworth House. Apart from everything else, the hotel is famous for its 10 miles of trout fishing on the Derwent and Wye. Fishing tickets are available, but a rod licence from the Severn Trent Water Authority is also required. The Devonshire Arms Hotel and the Wheatsheaf Hotel are also at this end of the village.

Return to the roundabout, by the Prince of Wales Hotel, and take the second exit marked "Stockport". Just round the corner is the church of St. Anne. It has an unusual clock face, erected to commemorate Queen Victoria's Diamond Jubilee in 1887. There is a Saxon cross shaft in the churchyard, from where the ancient stone bridge, with its mini toll-booth can be seen.

Continue along the A623, pass Cliff College, the Methodist Training Centre, to . . .

Calver and **Calver Sough.** ("Sough" means a drainage tunnel to a lead miner). Here the Derbyshire Craft Centre offers a comprehensive range of goods for the tourist, and they have a cafe. One of Arkwright's original mills stands here by the river Derwent. It now produces stainless steel sinks.

There are some good views of Froggatt and Curbar Edges from here. These are used for rock climbing, hill walking and hang gliding, as well as for flying model aircraft. There is a car park in Curbar Gap, at the top of Bar Road.

Continue along the A623 to . . .

Stoney Middleton, or just "Stoney" to the locals. The Romans built a bath here and there is a unique church building. Originally built by Joan Padley, as a thanks offering for her husband's safe return from the Battle of Agincourt, it is octagonal in shape. The village also contains the Moon Inn, a good chip shop and the Lover's Leap Cafe — so called after a young lady who threw herself off the nearby cliffs but was saved by her crinoline acting as a parachute. They have a village fete and the wells are dressed during the last week in July.

Further along the A623, opposite the quarry, turn right up the B6521 to . .

Eyam. "The Athens of the Peak", the village is famous for its writers and for the plague which arrived here in 1665. Five out of every six of the inhabitants died. The village takes its name from the Saxon word "EY" meaning water, and from "HAM" meaning a settlement. The wall of nearly every house and cottage in the village bears a small plaque giving details of the people who died here during the plague. Some give extra, less saddening, information about the village, and act as a guide in themselves.

Starting in the lower village square, find the Lydgate. It is by the red telephone box. There are several interesting items up here. The Lydgate Graves, recording the burial of a father and his daughter in 1666, are in a little croft on the right, just before the electricity pole. The plaque on No. 1 cottage explains the meaning of "Lydgate", and Fossil Cottage is up here. This was the home of William Wood, author and historian. His books included *The History and Antiquities of Eyam* and *Genius of the Peak and Other Poems.* Eyam's other writers include Anna Seward (the Swan of Litchfield), Rev. Peter Cunningham (curate and poet), Richard Furness (a gifted poet) and Clarence Daniel, who has his own private museum in the village (visits by previous arrangement, details on the church bookstall).

Return now to the square, called the Bull Ring. Another plaque on the corner of a shop on the top side of the square records the position of the metal ring to which bulls were tied, whilst being baited by the villagers' dogs. This was made illegal in 1840.

Go west now, up Church Street, pass the Glebe Fluorspar Mine, and find the church of St. Lawrence — a popular place for visitors. The churchyard contains a fine 8th century Saxon Cross, an elaborate sundial dated 1775 and the graves of Catherine Mompesson and Thomas Stanley. He supported the

Eyam Village (drawing by Sir Francis Chantry)

Rev. William Mompesson, rector of the village, at the time of the plague.

The story of the plague is well known — the people of Eyam decided to cut themselves off from the surrounding countryside to prevent the disease from spreading. They held their Sunday Services outside in Cucklett Delf as a precaution. A service is still held there every summer as a thanksgiving for the courage of the villagers.

Two ancient coffin lids have been placed close to the chancel doorway of the church. The top of one of these is known as "St. Helen's Cross" and can be seen inside the north aisle of the church. St. Helen was born in Derbyshire. The daughter of a Romano-British chief, she became the mother of the Roman Emperor Constantine. It is said that she found the remains of the cross on which Jesus was crucified. Part of this is now in Clarence Daniel's museum. There are some interesting brasses and hatchments inside the church, as well as the recently discovered wall paintings, dating from 1660.

Further along Church Street is the cottage where the plague began, the sheep-roasting spit, the village stocks on the Green and the Old Market Hall. There is a good map of the village on the wall of the market hall. Eyam Hall stands on the opposite side of the road from here.

Continue up the village to Hawkhill Road, also marked "Car Park". Pass the Methodist Church and the Youth Hostel, up to Eyam Edge, noting the view across the village towards the quarries above Stoney Middleton. Go round the bend in the road, and continue for about 100 yards towards Grindleford. Here, on the left, is Mompesson's Well, where food and medicines were brought during the plague and coins were placed under water in payment to the surrounding villagers, who kept them supplied. Ladywash Mine can be seen from here.

Return to the previous junction, and take the road marked Bretton, Great Hucklow and Abney. There are some marvellous views from up here — over the limestone to the left and the gritstone to the right. The road leads on to . . .

The Barrel Inn. A famous and lonely house, built in 1637, it is one of the highest pubs in England. John Wesley rode past here in a snowstorm after visiting Bradwell, on his way to Eyam Woodlands, in March 1765. There is a small Youth Hostel down the lane at the back of the pub. Stop here and listen for the sound of curlews. It is a peaceful spot.

Now continue along the hilltop and note the gliders at the Derbyshire and Lancashire Gliding Club's field above Abney. They have a large car park, but otherwise keep left at the next junction, and follow the sign to . . .

Great Hucklow. The Unitarians have their Holiday and Conference Centre here. Keep going along the B6049 as far as the Anchor Inn, cross the A623, and go into . . .

Tideswell, which takes its name from an ebbing and flowing well nearby. The church of St. John the Baptist is known as the "Cathedral of the Peak", and is rather a large building to be kept going by the township. It contains some good brasses and excellent wood carving in the chancel. William Newton, the "Minstrel of the Peak", is buried in the churchyard.

Sundial, Eyam Church

It is worth walking around the town. The First Drop Inn and Hunstone's wood carving shop are in the Market Square; Tideswell Dale Rock Shop and Tindall's pie shop are in the main street, opposite the George Hotel. Don Edwards, at the Rock Shop, has revived the ancient craft of inlaying coloured pieces into black Ashford Marble, once carried out all over the Peak from Buxton to Matlock. It is for sale in his shop, which is open from 9.30 am to 5.30 pm from Thursday to Sunday.

Keep going down through the town, along the B6049. There is a picnic site in the woods at the bottom of the hill, but turn left just before this, to Litton village. A quiet village street leads to a right turning marked . . .

Cressbrook and Monsal Dale. Note the limestone walls, typical of the White Peak, along here. Don't turn right, go round the hair-pin bend and down into the dale. Stop at Cressbrook Mill. Ravensdale, Monsal Dale and Millers Dale are all accessible from here, where the contrasts in the scenery can be appreciated. Continue through Monsal Dale and stop in the new layby just before . . .

Upperdale Farmhouse. A wonderful place to stay, where the farmer's wife provides excellent home cooking made from local recipes. Full details through the parlour window. (Note: This is where the Monsal Trail starts — see the recommended walk).

Climbing out of the Dale, there is another famous view from Monsal Head car park. As well as a very friendly pub, there is a craft shop, cycle hire shop and a cafe here.

Across the B6455, towards . . .

Great Longstone. There is a fine Georgian Hall here, where the Flemish weavers started a stocking industry in the 15th century. Turn left opposite the White Lion, who serve excellent meals, up Church Lane. Across the fields from Thornhill's Poultry Factory, Longstone Edge can be seen. This contains one of the world's largest deposits of fluorspar. The turn into Rowland is a cul-de-sac, so continue to . . .

Hassop. Here is the large Roman Catholic Church of All Saints. Their nativity crib is always placed outside at Christmas time, making a pleasant sight in the snow.

Hassop Hall is now a private hotel and restaurant, open to the public. The full history of the Hall, going back to the Doomsday Book, is printed on the back of their menus . . . it makes fascinating reading. It is a relaxing place after a day out, with a most enjoyable and friendly atmosphere.

Oppositie the Hall is the B6001 leading back to Bakewell which is only two miles away from here.

3. Bakewell, Buxton and Ashford

Bakewell — Monyash — Longnor — Buxton — Ashwood Dale — Taddington — Ashford-in-the-Water. 34 miles.

Recommended walks: "Circular Walks around Bakewell", by George Hyde.

STARTING outside the Rutland Arms Hotel, **Bakewell,** walk past Peter Rabbit's Bar, up North Church Street and round the corner, as far as the Gospel Hall on Oddfellows Row. Opposite here is a sign pointing to the Old House Museum. This is a 16th century house, now converted into a local history museum. It is open from Good Friday until the end of October from 2.30 to 5.00 pm each day. It contains timbered ceilings, some wattle and daub walling and large fireplaces. The exhibits are all from the Peak District and contain farmers' and miners' tools from past centuries. There is a display of Victorian costumes and lacemaking.

The pathway leads back towards the churchyard, which can be entered via the lychgate opposite the Parsonage. Note the Saxon cross near the church porchway, which contains a wealth of Saxon objects. There are almost thirty coffin lids, bearing various cross floree designs with swords, horns, a chalice, key and scissor motifs, each depicting the occupations of the deceased. Inside the church, which is dedicated to All Saints, is a 14th century font, a rood screen and an unusual memorial to Sir Godfrey Foljambe and his wife, dated 1377. Several musical events are held here during the year.

Now walk down South Church Street, which contains some fine antique shops. One of these, belonging to Michael Goldstone, is extensive and houses the finest collection of oak furniture, for sale, in Britain. There is a super bookshop "Bakewell for Books", on the corner with Matlock Street. Their three shops contain everything you could require in the way of guide books, general and second hand books, gifts and souvenirs. Browse around for your favourite titles, some of which are offered at bargain prices.

Further down the street is the Bakewell Pudding Shop, and cafe — just right for a morning coffee. Across Matlock Street is Granby Street, which leads to the cattle market. Walk through here to the general market, held on Mondays, in the square opposite the Peacock Hotel and the Queen's Arms. Call at the Peak District National Park Information Centre in the Old Market Hall. (More about Bakewell in Tours 4 and 5).

Return to the traffic island outside the Rutland Arms and take the B5505 to . . .

Monyash. This lies on the White Peak Scenic Route, which passes some fine looking Peakland farmsteads on the way. The villagers hold a market on Bank Holidays, and all the proceeds go to help third world countries. There is an antique shop at the top of Chapel Street and the church of St. Leonard contains a large 12th century oak chest.

Continue along the B5505 to the A515 Buxton to Ashbourne road. Cross this, taking the road towards . . .

Crowdicote. Note the fine view from the top of the hill above the village. A remarkable ridge separates the upper Dove Valley from the Manifold Valley beyond. Stop at the Pack Horse Inn, where bar snacks are served. The little bridge, at the bottom of the hill, crosses the Dove (more of this in Tour 7) into Staffordshire. The road then leads on to . . .

Longnor. Park in the Market Square and note the number of public houses around — also the Table of Tolls on the Market Hall. These include a toll of one penny for every pig sold there, payable to Sir Vauncy Harpur Crewe Bart, Lord of the Manor of Longnor . . August 1903.

Inside the Market Hall is Woodstringthistlefoss, a sculpture studio. Presently using clay to produce individual hand-made pieces, they intend to use all types of media in the future. Their products range from "The Wooden O", a model of Shakespeare's Globe Theatre, to their Moorland Series of figures, based on local characters and their animals. They also have a series of figures based on the Punch and Judy theme — all as good as the pieces made by the more famous factories, but at approximately half their prices. It is possible to see the modelling taking place, the first biscuit firing, the application of underglazes, further firings and all the other processes involved in the production of earthenware, procelain and china. They also make tile murals, cast in bronze and pewter, and will work in the local gritstone and alabaster. Open 9.00 am – 7.00 pm, seven days a week, during the summer.

The church of St. Batholomew has an interesting font, and the churchyard contains a most unusual headstone. This shows that the interned William Billings, amongst other things, was born in a cornfield and died at the ripe old age of 112.

Return to the Market Square, via a narrow village street containing the Parrott Restaurant. Constructed on the site of the Old Red Bull Inn, it now serves homemade cakes and cream teas everyday except Mondays.

Leave by the B5053 to Buxton. There are some even better views of the top of the Dove Valley, with Axe Edge on the left, from here. Cross over Glutton Bridge, back into Derbyshire, up the hill to the crossroads, and take the right turn to . . .

Earl Sterndale. Go a short way up into the village to see the pub. It is the Quiet Woman, as the headless figure on the inn sign would suggest. Back down to the crossroads, and turn right. This joins the A515, which leads to . . .

Buxton. Famous as a spa town since Roman days, when it was called Aquae Arnemetiae, and a place in which to enjoy yourself. It is very popular with holidaymakers and tourists and as a place for retirement. There is always something happening here, especially during the Festival, which takes place each year now at the end of July and into August. Call at the Information Centre in the Crescent for details of what is on at the time. It is open from 9.30 am to 5.00 pm everyday from April to October, and from 10.00 am to 12.30 pm and from 1.30 to 4.00 pm on weekdays during the winter season.

The main places of interest are:

The Opera House. Originally built in 1905, from a design by Frank Matcham in the grand Edwardian style, it seats almost 1000 people. It was used as a cinema for many years, but was restored and reopened as an Opera House in 1979, when the Buxton Festival began. It is magnificently decorated and contains one of the largest stages in England.

Pavilion Gardens. The Pavilion was built and the Gardens laid out in 1871 by Edward Milner, using money made available by the 6th and 7th Dukes of Devonshire. The Octagon Concert Hall was added later in 1875. The 23 acres of beautiful gardens, serpentine walks, decorative iron bridges and amusements for young and old make this the place to appreciate the real atmopshere of Buxton. A variety of events are held here, including book, antique and craft fairs, wrestling matches and band concerts. The River Wye flows through the gardens. The Conservatory was renovated and reopened in 1982 by Countess Spencer, chairman of the Spas Committee of the English Tourist Board. The Swimming Pool, in the Pavilion Gardens, is a new addition to the amenities. It is filled with warm Buxton Spa water, and is open most of the time. See the notice board outside.

Museum and Art Gallery. On Terrace Road, just before the Market Square, the museum contains some important items relating to the local history and geology of the area. This collection includes that of Sir William Boyd Dawkins and Dr. J. Wilfred Jackson, who added much to the understanding of local archaeology, and their study is preserved in the museum. They have a fine collection of Ashford Marble and Blue John ornaments, as well as paintings, prints, pottery and glassware. Open from 9.30 am to 5.00 pm, except Mondays.

The Library. This is in St. Anne's Crescent and is part of the buildings erected by the 5th Duke of Devonshire, from the profits made in the Ecton copper mines. It is well worth a visit just to see the elegant ceilings, especially the Assembly Room ceiling. This is above the upstairs library and was created by John Carr in 1784 for the 5th Duke of Devonshire. It is in the style of Robert Adam, and was Carr's masterpiece.

The Micrarium. Opposite the St. Anne's Hotel, they offer a unique display of microscopic plants, animals, minerals and preserved snowflakes. The marvellous displays open up the world of nature and can be easily operated by anyone. They are open every day from the end of March to early November, from 10.00 am – 5.00 pm. Well worth a visit.

Poole's Cavern and the **Country Park**. Back up the A515, through the Market Square to the traffic lights and up Green Lane. Pass Buxton College on the right, and then the entrance is on the left. The Cavern has been decribed as the finest show-case in the British Isles, and was used by the Romans and ancient man before them. It is entered horizontally, contains only 16 steps, is entirely lit by electricity and includes displays of various kinds. Grin Low Woods in the Park is a Site of Special Scientific Interest, containing some important flora, and Solomon's Temple is at the top of the wood, above the car park. This temple is really a folly built on the site of an ancient Neolithic burial mound, overlooking Buxton. It is named after Solomon Mycock, the farmer on whose land it stood.

Peak Rail Society have a depot at the Midland station. This is open on Sundays and Bank Holidays and on Saturdays during July and August. The Rambler steam train provides rides to New Mills and back, and the usual railways memorabilia is all available.

Spring Gardens. This is the main shopping centre, and contains some excellent shops, restaurants and coffee houses. Some of these stay open during the evenings.

At the end of Spring Gardens, go under the railway arch and take the A6 marked Matlock and Derby.

Ashwood Park. Alongside the A6, going south, offers a pleasant place to play bowls and tennis, and in which the children can play.

At the end of the gardens, take the A6 down . . .

Ashwood Dale. Go under the railway bridges, which Ruskin said "Took every fool in Buxton to Bakewell in ten minutes", up Topley Pike and turn right into the layby. There is an excellent view from here. Looking up Great Rocks Dale to the left, Eldon quarry, the largest in Europe, can be seen. To the right is Chee Dale, leading into Miller's Dale. Wormhill is on the far side. Continue along the A6, pass the Waterloo Hotel, and turn right into . . .

Taddington. A typical moorland village. Go down the main street as far as the church of St. Michael and All Angels. There is an interesting alabaster slab in the porchway. At Town End, take the road posted "Ashford". This goes down Taddington Dale. The bottom of Monsall Dale joins this dale, and the river Wye flows down here. Turn left into . . .

Ashford-in-the-Water. Probably best known for the black marble which is found in a quarry nearby, it is one of the prettiest villages in the Peak. The marble takes a high polish and was used to inlay coloured marbles, shells and glasses to produce the famous Ashford Marble, so popular in Victorian days. This was a thriving cottage industry and many beautiful pieces of work were produced.

There is a fine table top on show in the church of the Holy Trinity. This also contains their famous Maiden's Garlands, or Virgin Crants as Shakespeare called them in *Hamlet*. These were made whenever an

Ashford Marble

unmarried girl, or boy, was buried in the churchyard. They represent the lanterns carried by the wise virgins at the Wedding Feast mentioned in Matthew chapter 25, usually contained something which belonged to the deceased and were hung over their pew until the garland perished.

There is a tablet to the memory of Henry Watson of Bakewell, who started the marble works and wrote several books on the geology of the area. There are some pillars made from "Duke's Red", a rare marble only found in the Duke of Devonshire's mine in Lathkill Dale and now held in the cellars at Chatsworth House. The font is interesting and there is a Norman Tympanum over the south doorway.

The well dressings here are very popular, and the festivities begin with the blessing of the wells on Trinity Sunday.

Exchange visits between the people of Ashford and those from the Lazion town of Acquapendente in Italy, where they also make floral designs, have taken place in recent years.

A walk round the village should include Fennel Street and the Sheepwash Bridge over the Wye. Large brown and rainbow trout can be seen in the river, and are served at several places offering refreshment after a day out in the Peak.

Bakewell is just two miles further down the A6 from here.

4. Bakewell, Youlgreave and Flagg

Bakewell — Lathkill Dale — Youlgreave — Middleton-by-Youlgreave — Arbor Low — Flagg — Sheldon. 25 miles.

Recommended walks: "Youlgreave, Middleton and Alport", The Arkwright Society's Local History Trail No. 15.
"The Tissington and High Peak Trails", Peak District National Park 1980.

THE Rutland Arms Hotel, Bakewell, was built in 1804 as a coaching inn serving travellers between London and Manchester. It is the true home of the Bakewell Pudding, and also the place where Jane Austen revised her work *Pride and Prejudice* before it was published.

The famous pudding arose through a misunderstanding between the mistress of the hotel and a new cook. Mrs. Greaves showed the cook how to prepare her strawberry tart, which she always made for important visitors. The egg mixture should have been stirred into the pastry before the strawberry jam was spread over the top. but whilst Mrs. Greaves was welcoming her visitors, the cook made it the other way round. Fortunately, the guests enjoyed the "pudding" so much that Mrs. Greaves told her to make them all that way in the future.

Whilst staying at the hotel, Jane Austen so like the area that she decided to revise *Pride and Prejudice* before it was published. The revision included scenes at Chatsworth House, "Pemberley", and Bakewell itself, which appears as "Lambton". She used the hotel as the setting for two of the most romantic scenes in the book.

On the right, down Matlock Street, is Hebden Court. It is a paved courtyard, lit by old-style copper lamps, and is surrounded by small shops including a coffee room.

Take a walk round the Bath Gardens, so called after a Roman Bath discovered there. It was found near to the British Legion's Garden of Remembrance. The Duke of Rutland built Bath House nearby in 1697, to encourage tourists, but the town never developed as a spa. Further evidence of its antiquity, and of the Roman Bath, is that Bakewell, according to the West Saxon Chronicle (AD 924), was called Badecanwyllan — the Bathing Well. In 1330 the manor of Bakewell passed to Ralph Gernon, who obtained permission for the original market to be held in the town.

The High Peak Harriers meet in the district and have their kennels above the town, next to Lady Manners School. The local bye-laws prevent the

Conksbury Bridge, Lathkill Dale

driving of pigs through the town except on Mondays, Market Day — the busiest day of the week.

Take the B5055 up South Church Street, round the corner and then turn left up Yeld Road, not up Monyash Road. Continue along Yeld Road for about two miles, passing the right turn to Over Haddon, rounding the hairpin bends into . . .

Lathkill Dale. This can only be seen by walking along the pathway, through the green pasture by the still waters of the river. Note the fat brown trout, the wild peppermint, the kingcups and watch out for kingfishers. Further along, the thump of the water rams, using the force of the river to pump water up to the farms above, can be heard. Back to, and across, the bridge, round the corner to Conksbury Farmhouse, where refreshments are sold, take the left turn towards . . .

Youlgreave, or "Pommey" to the locals. Note the mineral workings on the right, and enter the village opposite the church of All Saints. The north wall of the church contains some of the fabric of the original Saxon church. There is an ancient font, unfortunately upturned and used to hold a sundial. This also stands on the top of the steps which once supported an ancient Saxon cross, now in the churchyard opposite the south doorway of the church.

The interior of the church is well worth seeing. There is an effigy of a knight in armour, thought to be John Rossington, and the alabaster table tomb of Thomas Cokayne, who died in 1488, is in the chancel. Note the Cokayne crest, a cockerel, around Thomas' helmet. The stained glass windows in the east end were made by William Morris from a design by Sir Edward Burne-Jones, the pre-Raphaelite artist. There is a delightful little brass, dated 1492, to Frideswide Gilbert. The nave contains a Norman font, compete with stoup, to hold the Holy Water to one side. This font once belonged to the chapel at Elton, not far away, and is the only one of its type in England. There is a figure of a pilgrim, holding a staff and a wallet, let into the wall on the north side of the nave. This may have been connected with the hermitage at Cratcliff Rocks nearby.

Cross over the main street to the George Hotel. This is a friendly pub, which proudly displays a portrait of the present Prince of Wales, who once popped in for a pint. Turn up the main street, by the Green Apple Tea-Room, to Hollands, the butchers. They make haggis, particularly useful to Scots abroad on Burns' night — but no-one brews the malt up here, yet. The Cooperative Store is now the local Youth Hostel and Thimble Hall is in the Market Square. This is the smallest Market Hall in the Peak, and is still used for selling goods on certain occasions.

The wells are dressed for the Saturday before the first Sunday before St. John the Baptist's day. There is a procession of decorated floats, festival queens from other villages and the local silver bands play.

Why do they call it "Pommey"? Some say that a pig once joined the village band, and it played "Pom- Pom- Pom" all the way down the village street, but the origin is more likely to be left over from the days when French prisoners, from the Napoleonic Wars, were made to work in the area.

Further up the main street, where the local shop kept up the old pre-decimal prices until quite recently, leads to the Farmyard pub, where bar snacks are served, and the locals gather. From here the road rises out of the village towards the High Peak Moors. Take the left turn to . . .

Middleton-by-Youlgreave. The road passes the top of Bradford Dale, and Middleton Hall is on the left, before entering the village. Lomberdale Hall is here. It is not open to the public, but was once the home of the celebrated Derbyshire archaeologist, Thomas Bateman, author of *Vestiges of the Antiquities of Derbyshire* (1848) and *Ten Years' Diggings* (1861). Some of his collection is now in the Weston Park Museum, Sheffield, and his memory still lives on. To his credit, Bateman had the neat little Congregational Chapel built in 1826, and he is buried in a field some distance behind this. His grave is appropriately marked by a modern "Bronze Age" urn, and is surrounded by iron railings.

Take the top road out of the village, marked "Newhaven". Then next right, along a lane marked "Monyash". Cross the crossroads, pick up the "White Peak Scenic Route" and follow this again, at the next junction. Pass the mineral workings in Long Rake Plantation and stop at the entrance to a farmhouse, standing high up on the left. There is a sign at the gate saying . . .

Arbor Low. This ancient henge is open to the public most of the time. After paying a small fee at the farmhouse, walk up their yard, through the stile and across a field to another stile, to the south-east. The first part of the earthworks to be seen is the mound. Go over to the notice, which gives some more details, and is sited at the northern entrance to the circle.

This is the second largest stone circle left in Britain. It was started about 5000 years ago in the Late Stone Age, and developed during the Bronze Age, 4000 years ago. It was used as an observatory and later as a festival site. On entering the circle, the stones seem to have been placed in twos before falling on their sides, but they probably never stood up. The circular mound, originally 20 feet above the ditch, gives some protection against the weather and is a clue to the name of the circle — Arbor Low means a "Sheltered Heap". This name probably also refers to a later burial site, placed on top of the mound, on the south side of the circle.

The entrance to Arbor Low

There is yet another burial mound to the south, called "Gib Hill". This is also a Neolithic burial site, taking its name from a gibbet which stood there in more recent times. There are some spectacular views from up here, where each hill top bears the remains of ancient chieftains.

Full of the bracing air, return to the roadway and continue left to the next junction. Turn left again here, leaving the White Peak Scenic Route to the right, turn left once again at the A515, and them immediately right, to pick up the High Peak Trail at . . .

Parsley Hay. Here is a car park, complete with cycle hire, toilets, picnic area, wardens, etc. An informative leaflet about the Trail is available at the office. After another bracing walk, rejoin the A515, going north. This is an impressive bit of Roman Road, leading from the Baths at Buxton towards Derby and Chester. Travel as far as . . .

Bull-in't-Thorn Inn. Built originally in 1472, this famous moorland pub offers bar snacks, a beer garden and a camping site. They welcome coach parties here.

Then turn right towards . . .

Flagg. A small moorland village, where the High Peak Harriers hold their Point-to-Point Races on Easter Tuesday. There is a caravan site here at the Elizabethan Flagg Hall, which is worth seeing. Take the road south marked "Taddington", passing two turns to the right, then turn right at the crossroads towards . . .

Sheldon. Note the fine views again, especially that of the Magpie Mine, just before the left turn into the village. Magpie Mine is owned by the Peak District Mines Historical Society, who show parties round by arrangement through their office in Matlock Bath. It is the finest preserved lead mining site in the Peak, and shows many of the techiques used by "The Old Man". This is an affectionate term used for the old miners, who in actual fact would have been young men in their day.

The church of St. Michael and All Angels is worth seeing.

It is a pity that the old Devonshire Arms is no longer there. They once tapped bitter ale from barrels and served it in stoneware jugs, whilst their customers sat on old monks' benches made from English oak, in front of an open fire.

Down the village now, left at the bottom of the hill, to "Ashford". Join the A6, and Bakewell is only two miles down the road from here.

5. Haddon, Birchover and Hartington

Haddon — Rowsley — Stanton-in-the Peak — Birchover — Winster — Pike Hall — Newhaven — Hartington — Alstonefield — Mildale — The New Inns. 30 miles.

Recommended walk: "The Tissington Trail", Peak District National Park 1980.

LYING alongside the A6, two miles south of Bakewell is another of the stately homes of England. It is the delightful . . .

Haddon Hall. Apart from being the best loved of all Derbyshire's great houses, it is the finest and most authentic medieval manor house in Britain. It is perfectly preserved, so much so that it has been chosen for the setting of several films.

The Hall, reached by a fairly steep uphill walk from the car park, predominatly bears the stamp of the 16th century. Its rooms and their settings, the warmth of the oak floors, panelled walls and old tapestries impart the air of an enduring home. Do not miss the beautiful Long Gallery, where the whole floor is said to have been cut from one tree, and the medieval kitchens with their wooden pens where the staff stood while waiting for orders.

Long held by the Vernon family, the Hall came into the possession of Sir John Manners, ancestor of the Duke of Rutland, when he married Dorothy, second daughter of Sir George Vernon, "King of the Peak". The story of their elopement is told in a book *Dorothy Vernon of Haddon Hall*, by Charles Major, published in 1916. It recounts their love for each other, and how Dorothy fled down the steps, on the south side of the Hall, on to John's waiting horse. The steps are known by her name today.

The grandeur seen today is due to the care and skill displayed by the 9th Duke of Rutland when he restored the Hall to its former condition and appearance at the beginning of this century. The Banqueting Hall and the Chapel must particularly be mentioned. The former is the oldest room in the Hall, its original structure is still substantially intact and it shows a typical medieval arrangement, dating from 1370. The chapel contains medieval wall paintings, a Norman font and a lovely memorial to Lord Haddon, who died when only a young boy. The centre light of the north window has the figure of the Virgin being taught to read by St. Anne, a theme which is also used in the wall paintings, dating from the early 1400s.

There is a Roman altar near the entrance to the Banqueting Hall. This altar was found near Bakewell many years ago, and it bears a Latin inscription which, when translated, says: "To the god Mars, Braciaca, Osittius Caecilianus, Prefect of the first Cohort of Aquitain, in performance of a Vow".

There are no guides, but a guidebook is sold at the entrance box. There is a bookstall and a cafe, but no dogs are allowed into the Hall or its grounds. Various functions now take place there throughout the summer, and the Hall may be hired for special occasions by arrangement with the Comptroller (telephone Bakewell 2855). The Hall is open from early April to the end of September, 11.00 am – 6.00 pm daily, except on Mondays and on Sundays during July and August.

Return to the car park, and travel south again along the A6. Don't take the B5056, carry on to . . .

Dorothy Vernon's Steps, Haddon Hall

Rowsley. Here is the Peacock Hotel, so called after the crest on the Rutland coat-of-arms. The hotel was originally built by John Stevenson, agent to Grace, Lady Manners, mother of the 8th Duke, and founder of the Bakewell School in 1652. The house later became a farm, and then, about 1820, an hotel. Longfellow stayed here, as did Maximilian, Emperor of Mexico, who came in 1867 before embarking on his fatal voyage. The hotel is well known today for its weekend breaks and as an anglers' venue. Rainbow and brown trout breed in the Wye nearby.

Caudwells' Mill is just across the road. It is one of the oldest water driven corn-mills in England. Still using this power, it produces a range of wholemeal flours, all of which are for sale in their shop. The flours are made on a unique set of roller mills installed at the beginning of this century. These can be seen working when the mill is open to the public. This is for about 20 days in the year, details of which are on the leaflets available in their shop. For party bookings on other days, please contact the Manager, Caudwell's Mill, Rowsley, Matlock, Derbyshire (telephone Matlock 734374).

Return to the village square, and take the byroad marked "Stanton-in-the-Peak". This leads down the village and over the bridge, passes the recreation ground on the left before climbing up the hill, Peak Tor. Note the fine view down Darley Dale on the left, cross the crossroads, and see another fine view, over Haddon towards Bakewell on the right. Keep going towards . . .

Stanton-in-the-Peak. Turn right down the hill, a short distance, and the Flying Childers public house is on the left. This was named after a champion racehorse owned by the 4th Duke of Devonshire. The church contains memorials to the Thornhill family, who lived at Stanton Hall.

Turn round, climb to the top of the hill to a layby, on the left, just outside the village. There is a fine view looking towards Youlgrave from here. Another layby, about a mile further along on the right, is opposite a track which leads onto Stanton Moor. This area is rich in archaeological remains, the whole area being inhabited from about 5000 BC. There are many ancient burial mounds, a standing stone, and the Nine Ladies Stone Circle. These are all protected monuments, and well worth seeing by walking around the footpath which circles the moor.

Further along this road are the stone quarries which produce high quality cut stone used for many famous buildings. Round the corner into . . .

Birchover. Among the usual village items is Marsden's Magic Stores, the Red Lion, which has a great country atmosphere, and the Druid Inn, where there is a restaurant.

Down to the bottom of the hill now and join the B5056 and the White Peak Scenic Route. Take the left turn towards Ashbourne. About one mile up here on the left is another layby, just before a sharp left-hand bend. Stop here and look directly across to the northern skyline — there is a most unusual rock formation which looks like a castle. It is Robin Hood's Stride, or Rowtor Rocks. A little further round to the east is Cratcliff Rocks where the hermit's cave is situated. Up to the crossroad now, and left along the B5057 into . . .

Winster. The main street contains antique shops, some interesting late 18th century houses and Winster Hall Hotel. At the top of the street is the Market House, now owned by the National Trust, who open it up as an Information Office between 2.00 and 6.00 pm. at weekends and on bank holidays. There is an annual Pancake Race here on Shrove Tuesday and a curfew bell is rung each night at 8.00 pm.

Return to the layby by the church of St. John the Baptist and enter the churchyard, via the gateway. There is a large gallery inside the church. The font must be seen — is it really Norman or was it a Tudor imitation? It looks as though it was only just carved, but the figures are certainly Norman. Llewllynn Jewitt, the famous Victorian antiquarian and local historian, lived at Winster Hall and is buried in the churchyard.

Back to the B5056 now, and left to the Miners' Standard. This well known pub was named after the Dish of Lead, or the standard measure of lead ore. Every time a certain amount of ore was produced in the local mines, one of these had to be paid to the landowner as a royalty.

Now follow the White Peak Scenic Route sign, the road marked "Elton". This is a Roman road; there is a field marked "Picnic Area" up the left turn to Elton, but carry on towards "Newhaven". Join the A5012, through Pikehall, where there is a proper picnic site three quarters of a mile down the lane to Parwich. There is a caravan site, complete with shop, just before the A515. Leave the White Peak Scenic Route here, and turn right at the Four Winds Cafe. Along the A515, take the next turn left — the B5054. Just before the bridge is a left turn to the . . .

Tissington Trail at Hartington station. This is described on the recommended walk. There are toilets, a picnic area and Park Wardens to assist, but no cycle hire at this point.

After a brisk walk, return to the B5054 and turn left, down the dale full of all kinds of wild flowers, down into . . .

Hartington. Famous as a tourist centre and for its Stilton Cheese factory, who show private parties around by previous arrangement. Their world famous product can be purchased at "Ye Old Cheese Shoppe", which looks like the newest building in the village. It is opposite the duck pond, not the Witches' Ducking Pool, which is at the side of the lane leading to the factory. A host of licensed restaurants and bed and breakfast houses surround the Market Square. There is the Charles Cotton Hotel, the Minton House Hotel and the Devonshire Arms Hotel in the square. The Sheepskin and Tapestry Shop offers a first class range of goods for the tourist.

The Youth Hostel must be seen to be believed. It is a 14th century manor house and farm — the ancient home of the Batemans. The inside walls, covered by oak panelling, are as impressive as the outside. Bonnie Prince Charlie is said to have stayed here in 1745, before setting out for Derby and his ruin.

The church of St. Giles is old, and contains some interesting relics. A long coffin slab in the south transept may be that of Margaret De Ferrers, Countess of Derby, and there is a small cabinet on the east wall of the transept. A notice under this says, "This qauntlet, believed to have come from Hartington Hall may have been worn by one of the Bateman family at the Battle of Agincourt 1415". However, the cabinet is empty, and another notice says, "This gauntlet was stolen in May 1983. If anyone can provide information leading to its recovery, the vicar and the church wardens would be pleased to hear from them". There are several little 18th century brasses on the walls which are worth seeing, even if they haven't been included in the lists of the more famous ones.

Back into the Market Square, take the road marked "Warslow" — the B5054. Go as far as the Staffordshire Moorlands sign, and stop at the Manifold Valley Hotel — a friendly place, where home-made traditional fayre is served in their "Valley Restaurant". The river Manifold flows under the bridge outside.

Turn left, before the bridge, along the road marked "Alstonefield and Wetton". Don't turn right to Ecton (where the copper mines are), but keep going. Look across to Ecton Hill on the right — the old copper mine workings can still be seen. Pass between the first and second of a row of sugar loaf shaped hills, typical of the topography around here and equal to anything seen on the White Peak Route. The Coach House Antiques and Craft Shop is on the left just inside the village of . . .

Alstonefield. Round the village green is the Smithy Caravan Site, the George Hotel, several houses offering bed and breakfast, Jean Goodwin's Studio — offering original oils and watercolours, and Ye Olde Post Office Stores and Tea-Rooms.

Leave the village on the road marked "Lode Mill", and go down into the top end of Mill Dale. Take the very sharp right turning down by the river Dove in Mill Dale. There is a delightful corner just before the bridge which takes the footpath down into the top end of Dovedale. There are toilets here, a good shop and several picturesque cottages.

Return to the first bridge in Milldale, continue along the road, back into Derbyshire, and take the left turn marked "Newhaven". This rejoins the A515 opposite the Alsop-en-le-Dale stop on the Tissington Trail. Turn right to the New Inns Hotel; they have 13 bedrooms and an interesting courtyard surrounded by stables converted into self-catering holiday flats, each one named after a local dale.

Ashbourne is only five miles further down — and Buxton 19 miles up — the A515 from here.

6. Matlock, Crich and Wirksworth

Matlock — Riber — Lea — Crich — Cromford — Wirksworth — Via Gellia — Matlock Bath. 32 miles.

Recommended walks:
"Walking in Southern Peakland", Peter Fooks (Walk No. 9, "Cromford and Bonsall").
"The High Peak Trail", 1981.

Matlock is a busy place, where a large number of bus services call at the bus station in Bakewell Road. There is a good covered market next to it.

All the major roads lead into Crown Square, near to the bridge over the river Derwent. Walk over this bridge and bear right into the car park. At the top of this is Matlock station, now the end of a British Rail branch line from Derby. Gone are the days when the "Blue Train" thundered through here on its way from Manchester to London, and vice versa. The age of the part-time enthusiast arrived here a few years ago, and the Peak Rail Society have taken over the old Ticket Office and Waiting Room. One is used as their shop and the other is used to hold an exhibition, explaining the history and intentions of the society. They are open from 10.30 am – 5.30 pm, seven days a week, for most of the year.

Walk back to the main road and look for the Book Cellar — it is just up the second road to the right. They have a range of new and second-hand books, some of which cover Derbyshire.

Back over the bridge now, and across the road into Hall Leys Recreation Park. A pleasant area in which there are some good floral borders, tennis courts, crown bowling greens, crazy golf, promenade walks by the river, a miniature railway, boating lake, children's paddling pool, swings and a slide. At the top end of the gardens, the Parish Church stands on a small hill, and Riber Castle stands out on the southern skyline.

The A615, towards Alfreton, passes the Ritz Cinema and Matlock Town Football ground, and soon leads into Matlock Green. Turn right, up Church Street, towards "Starkholmes", and stop at the church. This is the one which overlooks the gardens and it is dedicated to St. Giles — the patron saint of cripples, beggars and blacksmiths. A figure of the saint appears on the end of one of the stalls in the chancel. There is some rich carving on the pulpit and a fine stained glass window in the north aisle. This depicts Christ as the Good

Shepherd and as the Light of the World. The latter is after the famous painting by William Holman Hunt. There is an early font, described as Norman, but possibly Saxon, and the Wolley Tomb. This is under the west window of the south aisle, by the main doorway, and is an altar tomb to Anthony Wolley of Riber and Agnes, his wife. It is dated 1578, and bears the incised figures of the man, his wife and their six children. There is a cabinet containing six Maidens' Garlands on the wall to the left of the tomb (see Tour 3, Ashford-in-the-Water).

Return to the A615, and take the right turn to Tansley. Right again here, up Alders Lane towards . . .

Riber. At the back of this ancient village, on the edge of a hill overlooking Matlock, is Riber Castle. Originally built as a folly by John Smedley in 1852, this now houses the Riber Wildlife Park. The Park contains a large number of British and European birds and animals, including the world's best collection of lynx. Some of these have been supplied to the French Government, who reintroduced them into the Vosges Mountains in 1983. It is one the Rare Breeds Survival Trust's "Approved Centres", and houses some local rarities, such as Derbyshire Redcap poultry, as well as other endangered species. There is a large car park, cafe, souvenir shop and a new Nature Centre. Open from 10.00 am to 5.00 pm in the summer, and to 4.00 pm in the winter — only closed on Christmas Day.

Riber Hall, originally an Elizabethan manor house, is now an elegant hotel, offering luxury accommodation and an outstanding restaurant (telephone Matlock 2795).

Returning down the lane from Tansley, take the first right to Lea and Holloway. Across the fields to the east, the Sherwood Foresters' Regimental Monument can be seen on top of a limestone quarry face. Continue along this lane, taking two right forks, as far as Lea Main Road. Turn left here. Note the sign to Lea Rhododendron Gardens, pointing up Long Lane. These gardens were created out of an old quarry by John Marsden Smedley in 1935, when he began the task at the age of 68. They are well worth seeing in the late spring/early summer, when they are open to the public (telephone Dethick 380). Lea Green, the teacher training college and former home of John Smedley, is just by.

Next on the left is the Coach House licensed restaurant, tearooms, farm shop and craft workshop. They serve lunches and evening meals from 7.30 pm, except on Sundays (telephone Dethick 346).

Now take the road which leads to Tansley and Wessington, noting the picnic site in the woods on the left as you leave the village. Then take the second right, along Shuckstone Lane. There is a fine view across Derbyshire, Nottinghamshire and into Lincolnshire from a little further down here, and the Regimental Monument is now on the right. The fine views all around here can be seen by paying the small charge to go up the monument, which is open until 5.00 pm most days of the year.

The road now leads into . . .

The Tramway Museum, Crich

Crich. The church of St. Mary is worth visiting. Originally Norman, but rebuilt and extended in the 14th century, it contains a stone bible rest on the north wall of the chancel, and the tomb of Sir William de Wakebridge is in the north aisle.

The National Tramway Museum is at the top of the village. Founded in 1955, it is an open air working museum run by volunteer members of the Tramway Museum Society. There are about 40 trams from Britain and abroad, of which about a third are in working order. These provide rides along a mile of trackway, including a reconstructed early 1900s city street. Their special "Stop for Tea" ticket includes unlimited tram rides and an afternoon tea in the cafe. There is a large car park, and the museum is open at the weekends and on bank holidays from end of March to the end of October, from 10.30 am – 6.30 pm; and from 10.00 am – 5.30 pm on Mondays to Thursdays, from May Day to the end of September and on Fridays at the end of July and in August. The front of Robert Adam's Old Assembly Rooms building from Derby is here, and there are several other interesting items. Exhibitions are held at various times of the year, and party visits can be arranged (telephone Ambergate 2565).

Down the road through Wakebridge and into . . .

Holloway. A large house set in its own grounds on the left, Lea Hurst, now a private residential home, was the birthplace of Florence Nightingale.

Continue down to the bottom of the hill and drive along the road by the side of the Derwent. It was at a farmhouse along here that Alison Uttley wrote her books. These include *A Traveller in Time, Memories of a Country Childhood* and *Recipes from an Old Farmhouse*.

Just before the bridge, on the right, is the entrance to Willersley Castle, once the home of Sir Richard Arkwright but now a Methodist Guild Holiday and Conference Centre. Over the bridge and second on the left is the entrance to Cromford Meadows and the Cromford Canal. This is open at the weekends during the summer, when horses pull a passenger boat along the canal. The Leawood Pumphouse contains a unique beam engine dated 1849. The Wharf Museum contains a collection of stationary steam engines, and refreshments are served at the Meadow Close Tearooms. Details from the canal shop or from the Cromford Canal Society, The Old Wharf, Mill Lane, Cromford, Derbyshire (telephone Wirksworth 3727).

Stop a little further up the road, in the car park on the left opposite . . .

Cromford Mill. This was the world's first successful water-powered cotton-spinning mill. Built by Sir Richard Arkwright in 1771, it used the water from the Bonsall Brook and Cromford Sough, which drained a local lead mine. He acquired a second patent in 1775, built another mill on the site, and went on to build mills and houses for his family all the way up the Derwent Valley. Samuel Smiles devotes several pages of his *Self Help*, written in 1859, to this remarkable man. Cromford Mill now contains the Arkwright Society's shop, a cafe, a warehouse selling textile materials and an exhibition room. They are open from Wednesday to Sundays, but not on Saturdays during the winter. Guided tours and parties by arrangement (telephone Wirksworth 4297).

Just round the corner is the A6. Cross over this into **Cromford** itself. There is a small alleyway on the right, marked "Post Office". Scarthin Arts and Crafts Shop is up here, as well as the Boat Inn and Scarthin Books — a marvellous new and second-hand bookshop, which sells the book containing the walk recommended for this Tour, along with other documents, maps, postcards and music sheets. Open from 10.00 am – 1.30 pm and from 2.30 pm – 6.00pm, except Sunday mornings.

Walk round the dam, via "The Nick", and back into the square, where there is a blacksmith's shop. Now take the B5036 towards Wirksworth, noting the rows of stone-built cottages, some with three storeys, built by Arkwright for his employees. Just at the start of these, on the left, is **The Back Shop,** where Nicholas Malone paints local scenes in oils and runs a picture framing service. Leaning his boards on an easel under the oak beams in front of an old stone fireplace, he prepares his work for sale in his shop and for exhibitions at local events, such as Bakewell Show. The shop is open from 9.00 am to 6.00 pm on weekdays and on some Saturdays, when he is not at an exhibition.

At the top of the hill, on the left is . . .

Black Rock Picnic Site and an access to **the High Peak Trail.** This is satisfactory for a short walk, but leave a longer one for later. The site provides toilets, a picnic area and helpful wardens.

The B5036 then goes under the old railway bridge and down the hill into . .

Wirksworth. There is a exhibition put on by the local stone quarries on the left, just at the bottom of the hill. Further along, take the B5035, marked "Alfreton", but turn immediately left, down Cemetery Lane, where the Wirksworth Mill Shop sells a large range of mens, ladies, childrens and babywear at factory prices. Their customers come from all over Britain — the shop is open from 9.00 am – 5.00 pm daily.

Continue along this road, but cross over the Alfreton Road, by the George Hotel and park by the Post Office. There is a footpath just inside the churchyard, which leads to The Home of Frank Pratt, whose business specialises in the restoration and reproduction of antique furniture. His home was originally the Grammar School, founded in the 1500s, but it is now a workshop and a place to be seen to be believed. As the chips of oak, matured for nine years, fly from the planing machine and the smell of varnish hits the air, really beautiful pieces of fine oak furniture are created with great skill and affection. These will be the valuable pieces of antique furniture in the future, and a delight to see today. A large selection of these are in a separate showroom, but each piece is individually made to the customer's order. What a place to find, and from which to furnish your home.

The Parish Church of St. Mary is just in front of you now. This is another place to behold, as it was founded in 635 AD. Its special feature is the Saxon sarcophagus, believed to be that of the original Northumbrian monk, Betti, who was sent down by King Edwin to convert Mercia, under their King Penda. This tomb top was found under the floor of the chancel during some alterations made in 1820, but is now let into the wall in the north aisle of the nave. There is an interesting figure of a local miner going about his work, set into the west wall of the south transept, and many other items, which are well described in their guidebook.

Wirksworth is obviously an ancient place, as can be further seen by walking down their main street. There are some grand houses down here, and a 15th century cruck structure behind a public seat. George Eliot stayed here in the late 1850s and featured the town as "Snowfield" in her novel *Adam Bede*.

Walk back up the main street, along the lower side of the market square, round the corner to the right, towards the Library, but then across the road and up an entrance marked "Car Park". Follow the alleyway, in front of the United Reform Church, and up Chapel Lane. Go past the Temperance Chapel, 1860, and up to the **Moot Hall.** This was built by the direction of the Duchy of Lancaster in 1814, and is where the Barmoot Court is held. King John granted them the right in 1210 to settle all the affairs of the lead mining industry. These rights have been upheld ever since and still play an important role in the lives of the mineral workers in Derbyshire. The court

The Moot Hall, Wirksworth

sits in the spring and afterwards enjoys the hospitality of the Sovereign at the Hope and Anchor Inn.

Try to find your car again, through the maze of chapels and other popular meeting places in the town, and then take the B5023 to Middleton. This takes a left turn by the Lime Kiln Inn, and goes up the hill into . . .

Middleton by Wirksworth. Take the left turn towards Hopton, under the bridge and then two right turns to . . .

Middleton Top picnic site and engine house. This is run by the County Council and was originally built to haul wagons up the 1 in 8 gradient from the Cromford Canal. These wagons were then sent on their way, via the Cromford and High Peak Railway, to Whaley Bridge and then on again by another canal to Manchester. The engine worked for 134 years, until its retirement in 1963. It was then restored by volunteers, and can be seen working on the first Saturday in each month. The Engine House is also open on Sundays from 10.30 am to 5.00 pm. There is a visitor centre which tells the story of the Cromford and High Peak Railway, and cycle hire, picnic area, car park, information office, etc.

This is the place to pick up the **High Peak Trail,** well described in the recommended walk. Note the fine views to the south. Further details from the Head Ranger (telephone Wirksworth 3204).

Now return to the village, where D. H. Lawrence once lived at Mountain Cottage, and turn left. Travel through the village, over the top of the hill and down to meet the A5012 "Via Gellia" road, so called after the Gell family, who were said to have built a road up here to record their family's associations with the Roman occupation, many years before.

Turn right down the valley, passing a cottage, on the left, which is entirely made from tufa. This is produced when calcium carbonate, dissolved in the local waters, redeposits itself onto sand in the local rivers. Cromford is at the bottom of this road. Turn left up the A6 now, pass Masson Mill, built in 1769, and note the New Bath Hotel on the left. This is known for its indoor and outdoor thermal bathing pools, and is where Emperor Don Pedro II of Brazil stayed with his Empress in 1871. The road leads into . . .

Matlock Bath. It has:
- A large Tourist Information Office and the Peak District Mining Museum, in the Old Pavilion.
- Boating on the river Derwent.
- Venetian Nights and the Illuminations — from August Bank Holiday weekend into October.
- Derwent Gardens and Lovers' Walks.
- Temple Mine.
- Model Railway Museum.
- Excellent fish and chip shops.
- Gulliver's Kingdom.
- The Fishpond and the Fishpond Hotel.
- The Petrifying Well, where even a bird's nest has been turned into stone.
- North Parade, where a string of shops offers everything a visitor could ever need.

Round the corner, on the road back to Matlock, is the bottom end of the new cable car system, serving the Heights of Abraham, Victoria Prospect Tower and the Rutland Cavern, referred to as "The Nestor Mine" in the Doomsday Book.

Matlock itself is two miles further up the A6 from here.

7. Ashbourne, Tissington and Dovedale

Ashbourne — Fenny Bentley — Tissington — Thorpe — Dovedale — Ilam — Wetton — Winkhill — Alton Towers — Denstone — Norbury. 50 miles.
Recommended walks: "Walks around Dovedale" — Peak National Park Walking Guide No. 3.

Ashbourne, the "Gateway to Dovedale", is full of history. It was one of Dr. Samuel Johnson's favourite places. He and Boswell came here, to stay with their friend Dr. Taylor at the Mansion House several times between 1737 and 1784. There is a chair at the Green Man and Black's Head Hotel in St. John's Street, which still bears the doctor's name, and there are many parts of the town which have not changed since his day.

George Eliot described the church of St. Oswald as "the finest mere parish church in the kingdom". (More abour her later). It was consecrated in 1241, has a spire over 200 feet high and is very impressive. There are several chapels inside, including the Boothby Chapel. Here lies Thomas Bank's famous sculpture of Penelope Boothby, who died in 1791, at the age of 5. The sculptor captured her innocence, which is also immortalised by Sir Joshua Reynolds when he painted her portrait two years beforehand. She became even more famous when Sir John Everett Millais painted his "Cherry Ripe" portrait of a young Miss Talmge, who had been to a fancy dress party as "Miss Penelope".

There is a canopied tomb of Robert de Kniveton, who died in 1471, and some fine stained glass in the windows. The oldest glass is the set of 13th century nativity medallions in the north transept — note the one depicting the angel appearing to the shepherds. The almshouses, in the churchyard, were set up by Nicholas Spalden, whose plate is on the west wall of the south transept.

Walking back along Church Street towards the town centre, note the Elizabethan Grammar School on the left. This was founded by Sir Thomas Cokayne but no longer houses the school. On the other side of the road is the Mansion House. This was the home of Dr. Taylor, who was at school in Litchfield and later an undergraduate at Oxford with Dr. Johnson. There is an unusual inscription over the doorway. Church street still contains many other elegant houses, mostly antique shops now, but there is a shop which specialises in prints.

The Green Man and Black's Head, Ashbourne

Looking up St. John's Street, the Green Man, which once combined with a small posting house called the Black's Head, a little further up the strret, now sports an inn sign which hangs right across the street. The hotel is well equipped and Dr. Johnson and his friends would still be comfortable here today. The Tourist Information Office is just round the corner in the Market Square, which is now a Conservation Area. What remains of Ashbourne Hall now acts as the public library. The Hall was the seat of the Cokayne and later the Boothby families. Bonnie Prince Charlie stayed here on his way to, and on his way back from, Derby in 1745. Don't miss the Ashbourne Gingerbread Shop, on the lower side of the market square.

The town is famous for its Shrovetide football match. This is a free-for-all struggle between the Up'ards and the Down'ards, being those who live on each side of the Henmore Brook which runs through the town. The brook is part of the field of play and the goals are Struston Bridge and Clifton Bridge, three miles apart. There are no rules, but some respect is paid to life and property. Various celebrities are asked to start the game each year.

There is a swimming pool, some squash courts and cycle hire in the town.

Leave by the road up the hill, marked "Dovedale". This is the A515, which passes the Bowling Green Inn at the top of the hill. Don't turn off to

Thorpe, but note the caravan site, with a shop, on the right, just past the turning to the left. Continue towards Buxton, passing Bentley Brook Hotel on the right, and go down into . . .

Fenny Bentley. A picturesque village with the Coach and Horses public house, the old Hall and its church of St. Edmund. This contains some 16th century screens and a most unusual tomb. It is Elizabethan. Made from alabaster, it depicts Thomas Beresford with his wife Agnes and their sixteen sons and five daughters, each covered by a shroud. The father and eight of his sons, along with some of their retainers, formed a complete troop of horse at the Battle of Agincourt in 1415.

Regain the A515, turning left up the hill, passing another caravan site on the left, under the old railway bridge. Turn right at the crossroads, just after the Blue Bell Inn, into . . .

Tissington. The first well dressings of the year are held here on Ascension Day. The Hall, the Town, the Yew Tree, the Hands and the Coffin Wells are all decorated with flowers from the area, each one depicting a scene from the Bible. The wells were dressed here as far back as 1350, and possibly before that.

The Old School Tearooms are open from 2.30 to 5.30 pm each day, and from 11.00 am to 1.30 pm as well during the school holidays and on Bank Holidays. They serve coffees and cream teas.

The church of St. Mary stands well on a rise overlooking the village and contains many memorials to the Fitzherbert family. The font is very interesting. It is tub shaped and was made to go in the original building, built here in Norman times — note the archway into the chancel. There are some old hatchments and the pulpit is unusual. It has been converted from a 'double-decker" type, which once had its own steps leading out from the priest's stall below.

The Hall, which dates from the 17th century, is the home of the Fitzherbert family, who have lived here for the last 500 years or more. There was an older Hall, which stood on the other side of the road. The present Hall is not open to the public.

To the left at the bottom of the village is a sign pointing to the Tissington Trail. This is on the site of the old railway station, where there is ample car parking space, toilets, ice-creams, tea, coffee, a picnic area and helpful wardens. Take a walk up here, or wait for a better one later. Bent Farm, offering bed and breakfast, is up here on the road to Bradbourne.

Returning to Old School House, take the same road, marked "Dovedale", out of the village, through the avenue of lime trees, to the A515. Cross the main road towards Thorpe. There is a car park on the left, just before the Dog and Partridge. Turn right here. At the top of the hill, on the right, is the pyramid-shaped Thorpe Cloud Mountain, and at the bottom of the hill is the Peveril of the Peak Hotel. This is now a large hostelry with 41 bedrooms and a car park for 100 cars.

The village of Thorpe contains several bed and breakfast houses and has a picturesque church to the left of the village green. There is another large car park — somewhere to leave the Land Rover when hang-gliding in the area and ideal for school party transport. Accommodation, with a licensed restaurant, is offered at Hillcrest House, just before going down the hill into . . .

Dovedale. After the small bridge over the Dove, turn right and then left to the Izaak Walton Hotel. Originally a 17th century farmhouse, most of the character has been preserved in the extensive renovations which have been carried out to make this 33 bedroom hotel such a delightful place to spend a holiday or just for a weekend break. Each room is equipped with all the modern comforts and the hotel is the nearest to the famous dale. This can be seen from the garden, or better still by returning down the drive and turning left up the lane.

There is a large car park, toilets and a tea bar here, which is on one of the recommended walks. Just a stroll up to Milldale and back will show the beauty of the dale. Visited and sung about by many poets, Dovedale is probably the best known for the delights of its fishing in times past. This was well recorded in *The Compleat Angler* written by Izaak Walton and Charles Cotton, whose Fishing House is still preserved in Beresford Dale.

Afterwards, turn back down the lane and turn right. There is a coach park on the right of this lane, which takes you into the Staffordshire Moorlands area of the National Park and then into . . .

Ilam. The Market Cross, although splendid, is mid 19th century and was erected by Jesse Watts-Russell in memory of his wife. He was an industrialist who bought the Ilam estate around 1818. He rebuilt the Hall, which is now owned by the National Trust but mostly occupied as a Youth Hostel. There is a car park, tearoom, gift shop and an official Caravan Club camping site with a shop.

The parish church of the Holy Cross contains several interesting items, including the Chantry Chapel. This was built to house Chantry's sculpture of David Pike Watts on his death bed, blessing his daughter and her three children. The Chapel of St. Bertram, a local Saxon prince whose family was eaten by wolves in the 9th century, contains the lid from his tomb. This became the object of many medieval pilgrimages. The Chapel also contains a painting of St. Helen taking the Holy Cross to Constantinople, after she had found it in 326 AD. They have two Maidens' Garlands and an important Saxon font in the nave, as well as several Saxon cross shafts in the churchyard.

The area around Ilam reminded Mr. Watts-Russell so much of Switzerland that he rebuilt most of the cottages in the village in a Swiss style. Even the school was modelled in this fashion.

Leave by the road which passes the school and is marked "Alstonefield". There is a good view of the Manifold Valley to the left and several farms offering official camping sites for caravans and tents. At the top of the hill, the appropriately named Air Farm offers bed and breakfast. On entering Stanshope, note the view of Ecton Hill to the north and turn left towards "Wetton" at the next junction. There is a better view of Ecton Hill and of the hamlet of Hope, to the right, from here. The road leads into . . .

The Chantry Chapel, Ilam

Wetton. At the top of the village is the Olde Royal Oak Hotel. This is a free house offering bar snacks with your drinks. They have a camping site and a large car park. Nearly all the farms sell ice-cream, minerals etc.

Turn right at the bottom of the village, along the road marked "Grindon". More camping sites and a toilet block here, before turning right along the road marked "Wetton Mill". Left at the next junction and down the single track road with passing places.

The spectacular sight of Thor's Cave is on the left, and the spire of Grindon church can be seen in the background. The cave is high above, and was carved out by water long before the valley became so deep. It can be reached by a path and some steps. This, and the other caves around here, were first used by Prehistoric man. Down in the valley, the footpath is taken to the left by a wooden bridge over the river Manifold, and to the right by a lane and a small stone built bridge. The roadway follows the track of the old Manifold Railway to . . .

Wetton Mill. This old corn mill closed in 1857 and is now owned by the National Trust, who have a shop and a cafe here.

At the bottom of the valley, near Darfar Bridge, in dry weather the river disappears and flows for five miles underground through a series of caves and fissures before reappearing at the Boil Hole in the Country Park at Ilam.

Opposite the mill, the second road to the right, not the road through the ford to the left, is marked "Butterton". This road climbs steeply and provides good views of the top end of the Manifold Valley. Watch out for oncoming traffic, and use the passing places. Note the two church spires of Grindon and Butterton to the left. Turn left into . . .

Butterton. A moorland village, containing some delightful cottages and the Black Lion Inn, built in 1782 (telephone Onecote 232). Turn down here and join the road from Onecote. Left, through the long ford, and up the hill past the farm selling goat's milk. Bear right at the junction and then turn left, before bearing right again at the next junction towards "Waterhouses". Right again towards "Waterfall", and then right again to "Winkhill". The next junction is marked A52; turn left towards "Ashbourne".

A few miles down here is Waterhouses and the George Hotel, and a fish and chip shop. Turn right by the Old Crown towards "Cauldron". Just under the bridge, on the left, is the Peak National Park cycle hire, car park and picnic site. The trail leads to the Hamps and Manifold track. Continue up the road, past the Blue Circle Cement factory, into . . .

Cauldron, where there is the Yew Tree Inn. Crossing the A52, pick up the signs to "Alton" and "Ellastone". Turn left at the next junction, noting the fine views over all of Staffordshire. Take the right turn at the B5417, and just past the Spar Caravan Site turn left opposite the Olde Star Inn. This leads into . . .

Alton Towers. Now Europe's premier leisure park catering for millions of visitors each year, these gardens were originally laid out by the 15th Earl of Shrewsbury in 1814. The entrance fee includes car parking and all the 70 attractions in the park, which covers 800 acres. Alton Towers is open every day from the end of March to the beginning of November.

Down the road now into Alton village, where Alton Castle, with its fairytale look, is perched on a hilltop overlooking the valley. The castle is now St. John's preparatory school for boys. Take the B5032 towards "Cheadle", passing the Wild Duck Inn on the left. Bear right, noting the old lock-up in the Square. Go up Limekiln Lane leading towards "Uttoxeter", and join the B5032 again, leading to . . .

Denstone. This is the home of Denstone College, one of the Woodard public schools. Then take the road towards . . .

Rocester. The road has now been re-routed to accommodate the huge J.C.B. excavator factory. Very well landscaped with a helicopter pad, this factory has developed very quickly over the last 20 years.

Cross the B5030 into the village. There was a Roman camp here, and the outlines of this can still be seen near the church, which has some fine windows. One of these contains ten scenes from the life of Christ by William de Morgan. There is an excellent Saxon cross shaft in the churchyard.

Take the road over the Dove, towards "Marston Montgomery", which passes Abbotsholme School on the right. Left at the next crossroads, through Roston village, to . . .

Norbury. Turn right at the B5033, and go up the hill to the church, which is by the side of Norbury Manor. The Manor, once the home of another branch of the Fitzherbert family, was enlarged during the reign of Queen Anne and is still a private house.

The church of St. Mary and St. Barlok contains a large amount of ancient stained glass and the chancel is magnificent. It contains the Fitzherbert tombs, carved by English medieval sculptors who worked from the beginning of the 14th century until the Reformation. Time doesn't move very quickly here, but it has left its mark on the fabric and windows of the church. These have recently been altered and restored, following a fund-raising campaign. Money is still required to complete the operation.

Note that the churchyard contains several yews, which provided the wood for archers' bows, and that there are the marks on the south wall of the church left by these men when sharpening their arrows.

Also note Norbury's connection with George Eliot and Adam Bede. George Eliot's maiden name was Mary Ann Evans, and she based the character of Adam on her father Robert Evans. He was born in the parish of Norbury in 1773, sang in the church choir and is said to have made the alter in the Lady Chapel. His parents, George and Mary Evans, are buried in the churchyard.

Return to the B5033 and take the left turn to Clifton, a small village where the pub is called The Cock, after the Cokayne family crest. At the top of the village is the A515, which leads back into Ashbourne.

Index

Alstonefield, 33
Alton Towers, 46
Arbor Low, 27
Ashbourne, 41
Ashford-in-the-Water, 22
Ashwood Dale, 22
Austen, Jane, 24
Bakewell, 12, 19, 24
Bamford, 9
Barrel Inn, 17
Baslow, 14
Birchover, 31
Brough, 9
Butterton, 46
Buxton, 21
Calver, 15
Castleton, 9
Cauldron, 46
Caverns, 11
Chatsworth, 14
Cressbrook, 18
Crich, 36
Cromford, 37
Crowdicote, 20

Denstone, 47
Derwent Valley, 9
Dovedale, 44
Earl Sterndale, 20
Edensor, 13
Eyam, 15
Fenny Bentley, 43
Flagg, 28
Great Hucklow, 17
Great Longstone, 18
Haddon, 29
Hartington, 32
Hassop, 18
Hathersage, 6
Holloway, 37
Hope, 9
Ilam, 44
Ladybower, 8
Lathkill Dale, 25
Longnor, 20
Longshaw, 6
Matlock, 34
Matlock Bath, 40
Middleton-by-Wirksworth, 39

Middleton-by-Youlgreave, 26
Middleton Top, 39
Monsal Dale, 18
Monyash, 20
Norbury. 47
North Lees, 8
Parsley Hay, 28
Peveril Castle, 10
Pilsley, 12
Riber, 35
Rocester, 47
Rowsley, 31
Sheldon, 28
Stanton-in-the-Peak, 31
Stoney Middleton, 15
Surprise View, 6
Taddington, 22
Tideswell, 17
Tissington, 32, 43
Tramway Museum, 36
Wetton, 45
Winster, 32
Wirksworth, 38
Youlgreave, 25